Louis Harris – Carla Tyler

HOW TO PLAY

HARMONICA

IN EASY WAY

A Complete beginner's Guide illustrated Step by Step.

Features, Easy Instructions, Practice Exercises

to Learn How to Play the Harmonica

Copyright © 2020 publishing.

All rights reserved.

Author: Louis Harris

No part of this publication may be reproduced, distributed or transmitted in any form or by any means, including photocopying recording or other electronic or mechanical methods or by any information storage and retrieval system without the prior written permission of the publisher, except in the case of brief quotation embodies in critical reviews and certain other non-commercial uses permitted by copyright law.

Table of Contents

Introduction 5

Harmonica Anatomy 7

Harmonica Types 10

Bending 18

You Can Easily Learn to Play The Harmonica 22

Know your Harmonica 24

Music Notation with Tablature 27

Blowing a harmonica/How to Hold Your harmonica 31

Techniques for Playing 39

How To Play The Diatonic Harmonica In The Key of C: 45

Frequently Asked Questions 47

Introduction

The harmonica is a free-reed wind musical instrument, played by blowing or drawing air through one or more gaps. Other names for the harmonica are harp, blues harp, mouth harp, hand reed, Mississippi saxophone, or pocket sax.

The main harmonica was made 1824 at Vienna from Anton Reinlein and Anton Haeckel. In 1857 Matthias Hohner was the first to mass-produce harmonicas and make the Hohner Company, the industry chief in reed instruments to date. In 1924 Hohner made the chromatic harmonica. The harmonica got mainstream during the 1950s, that it was presented in the blues music.

Today the harmonica is utilized generally in blues and people music, yet in addition sounds incredible for rock, old style, and tango music.

This technique plans to assist one with figuring out how to play the harmonica without an instructor. In contrast to most harmonica techniques, it doesn't focus on a particular music genre.

Information on fundamental music theory is required to ace this strategy. However, this strategy utilizes the sheet music documentation framework, being a lot simpler for the amateur to peruse than present day documentation.

For this technique, we will utilize the 10-opening diatonic harmonica in C, the most well-known harmonica for harmonica learning. In the wake of finishing the strategy you ought to have the option to play any harmonica. It is prescribed that you utilize the Hohner Marine Band harmonica in C, the most exemplary harmonica, with an unmistakable sound and standard shape and size, making it perfect for learning and excellent for show playing.

Harmonica Anatomy

The harmonica comprises of three fundamental parts, held together with screws or nails:

The cover plates: the covers that ensure you can't arrive at the reeds while playing and shield the harmonica from outer perils. Open back cover plates produce a splendid and clear sound. Also, open sides make the sound considerably more brilliant. Full cover plates produce warm and full sound, useful for Mississippi blues, country, jazz, and old style music. Metallic plates produce a splendid sound. Plastic plates produce delicate plastic sound. Wooden plates produce a delicate clean sound.

The reed plates: the metallic (regularly copper) platters that fill in as represents the reeds. The reeds are the meager metallic strips that create sound by vibrating when you blow or draw air at the gaps of the harmonica. The plates have little gaps in the size of the reeds, called spaces, that fill in as aides for the air that originates from the chambers. Broken reeds require full reed plate substitution.

The comb: the biggest piece of the harmonica, most usually wooden, fills in as host for the chambers through which air will be guided to the reed plate spaces, lastly to the reeds. Wooden combs produce more warm, perfect and original sound than other materials, however swell with dampness and salivation. Plastic combs don't endure dampness impacts and are light. Plexiglass combs permit you to see through the harmonica, making it simpler to know when your harmonica requires cleaning. Metal (normally aluminum) combs sound like plastic however are more overwhelming and sturdier.

A few harmonicas, for the most part chromatic ones, have valves (additionally called "wind savers") appended to their reed plates, that keep air from going through unused reed openings, giving more air to the objective reed. These valves used to be made of leather, yet these days are made of a slight plastic strip or pair of strips.

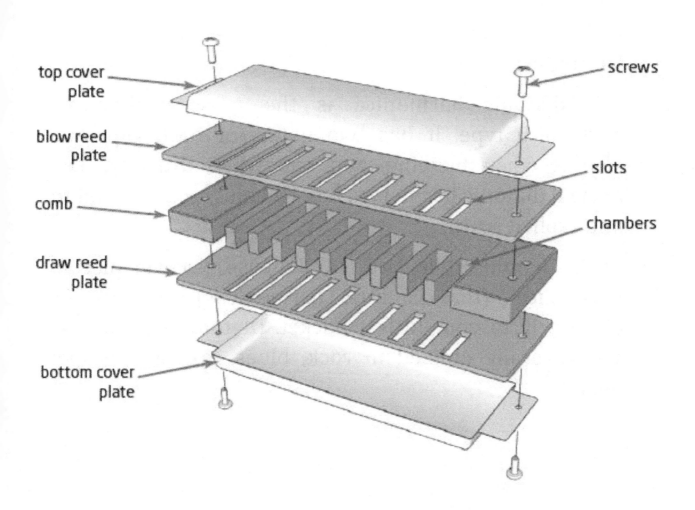

Harmonica Types

There are a few harmonica types, each with it's own unique sound and capacities.

Diatonic

The diatonic harmonica is the most well-known harmonica type. It has two notes for each gap: one sounds when blowing, and one when drawing. The normal diatonic harmonica has 10 holes, and is tuned to one explicit scale.

In the diatonic style, you will likewise discover piccolo harmonicas (that is, little harmonicas) that can fit effectively to your littlest pocket. Diatonic harmonicas are generally utilized in rock, blues, jazz and gospel music.

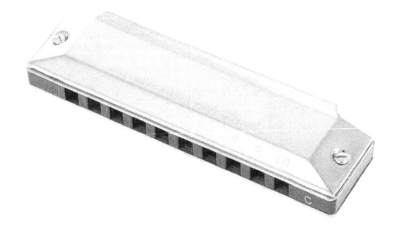

Chromatic

Chromatic harmonicas have four notes for every gap, and a side catch. At the point when the catch isn't squeezed, each gap sounds one diatonic note when blowing and one when drawing. At the point when the catch is squeezed, the notes become sharp. This permits you to play the entire chromatic scale. Chromatic harmonicas are generally utilized in old style and tango music.

Tremolo

Tremolo harmonicas have two columns of holes. Each opening produces just one note, eather when blowing or drawing. When playing, you drive air through both the upper and lower line of holes. The two holes produce a similar note, yet one is somewhat tuned away from the other, creating a warm vibrating impact.

Tremolo harmonicas are for the most part utilized in society (Celtic, Irish, and so on) music.

Octave

The octave harmonica resembles the tremolo, however it has a banana-like shape. The lower push is tuned an octave higher that the upper one, creating a solid sound.

Orchestral

Orchestral harmonicas have an assortment of styles, explicitly intended for orchestral playing. There are chord harmonicas intended to play chords, or chromatic harmonicas with all notes and semitones in succession (without button). These harmonicas are generally helpful in great outfits.

How the Harmonica Works

If you somehow happened to blow into the holes of a harmonica, individually from left to right, you would hear the 1, 3, and 5 notes of a major chord (C, E, G in the key of C) rehashed multiple times (just as one high C toward the end). Alone, this won't help you a whole lot, as it's just one chord.

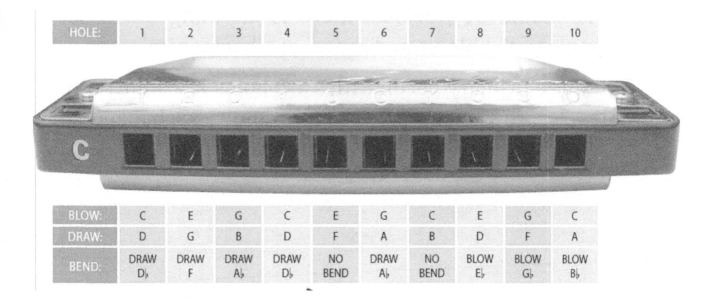

That is the reason playing the harmonica includes a combination of inhaling and breathing out (likewise called blowing and drawing). On the off chance that you blow into opening four on a C harmonica, you'll hear a C. Presently breathe in the note climbs to a D. Blow into the following gap and it's an E. Breath in, F. Blowing into gap 6 creates a G, and inhaling makes an A. Now you can likely think about what come straightaway on the off chance that you blow into gap 7: a B, isn't that so? Wrong! On the off chance that you blow into opening 7, you will hear a C. You need to breathe in to deliver the B. As should be obvious, there is anything but a set example to the blows and draws of a harmonica.

The three primary peculiarities are holes 2, 7, and 10. In holes 7-9, the example referenced above is changed so inhaling moves the note down rather than up.

How the Harmonica Produces Sound

There are 20 reeds on the harmonica 10 on the blow (breathe out) reed plate and 10 on the draw (breathe in) reed plate. Both reed plates are joined (generally using screws) to a comb (usually made of wood) where the air is directed through each reed in turn. Blowing through Hole #1 vibrates and sounds the blow #1 reed (C on a C Harmonica) and drawing through a similar opening vibrates and sounds the draw reed (D on the C Harmonica). Cover plates give the harmonica player a surface to hold the instrument without upsetting the vibration of the reeds.

The "cushion" side of the reed as it is known in the harmonica network, is connected to the reed plate (generally with a bolt). The "tip," or free-finish of the reed, leave the reed opening (upward swing) and discharges a "puff" of air. The reed then reenters the space (descending swing) and afterwards begins the upward swing again to release another puff of air. Each puff makes a weight wave, of which there are roughly 262 for the number #1 Blow reed on the C Harmonica to create the pitch C4. The closer the resistances between the reed and its opening (both draw and blow reeds), the more of the player's air goes towards tone creation.

To see how bending works on the harmonica, the pitches of both blow and attract reeds should be mapped—the two reeds are engaged with the bending procedure. Point by point in Figure 4 are the notes of the C Major Diatonic Harmonica.

Bending

Bending is difficult to get from the outset, however simple to do once you get it. Notwithstanding, this isn't an apprentice procedure. Ensure you can do everything referenced already, particularly playing single notes, before you endeavour twists.

Bending is utilized to change the pitch of a note. While inhaling or breathing out, you change the state of your mouth, changing the speed at which the reed is vibrating and the pitch of the note that plays. Twists are essentially utilized when playing blues harmonica.

The most widely recognized twists are draw twists, particularly on the lower notes. Nonetheless, there are likewise blow twists, overblows, and overdraws.

Presently to the genuine procedure. Bending is exceptionally difficult to clarify in words, so I will cite from some online tutorials. Make certain to look at this site for point by point guidelines on the most proficient method to twist each gap and some extremely pleasant activities.

Playing "twists" utilizing the TILT Method.

Start with the #4 draw (you can pick any note, to begin with however the general agreement is by all accounts that #4 draw is most straightforward). Recall that you should change the point of the wind stream over the reed to "twist" the note. So how about we cheat a tad and adjust the edge of the harmonica rather than modify the wind stream point by changing your mouth, tongue, and throat. Hold the harmonica by the closures and afterwards while playing a clean #4 draw. Tilt the rear of the harmonica up towards your nose. Ensure that when you tilt the harmonica up that you keep on drawing the air through the harmonica; however, you hadn't tilted it up.

- Do not let your head, mouth, and tongue follow the edge of the harmonica with your airstream, or you discredit the impact of tilting the harmonica in any case.

- REMEMBER: You should change the edge of the wind stream over the reed to make the note twist. This stunt of truly tilting the harmonica up will make a similar difference in point that you should, in the long run, figure out how to do with your mouth, tongue, and embouchure. If the harmonica jumps out of your mouth, begin once again and ensure you have the harmonica set far enough into your mouth with the goal that it won't jump out.

- TILTING TIPS: The reed in each opening requires an alternate edge to accomplish a twist. As a rule, these edges resemble this:

Gap #4 draw takes around a 45-degree change of wind stream edge.

Opening #2 draw takes very nearly a 75 to 90-degree change of current wind edge

To get it to twist down an entire advance.

Gap #3 draw takes a point someplace in the middle of 45 and 90 degrees.

Test with the tilting method until you get an adjustment in pitch. At the point when you begin getting a "twist" remain with it until you can roll out a perceptible improvement in pitch. On the off chance that you just can't get #4 attracted to "bend"....go ahead and attempt an alternate opening. If one practice meeting doesn't yield any "twists", consider it daily and return tomorrow. In any case, whatever you do, don't surrender.

You Can Easily Learn to Play The Harmonica

The chance that you'd prefer to figure out how to play the harmonica the best thing you can do is to take one. Despite the fact that there are several projects offering sheet music and guidelines, perhaps it would be better for you to begin probing your own as playing the harmonica isn't generally hard. You can begin your own and later get formal guidelines from different harmonica experts.

You stick up to my recommendation, and you'll get what's extremely significant - your own thoughts and comprehension of the instrument. I, for one, figured out how to play the harmonica around seven years prior and more often than not, I was probing my own. However, I confess to having utilized some formal guidelines occasionally, as well. As the harmonica is spread out in a natural manner, figuring out how to play it without anyone else is certifiably not a troublesome assignment, and it's worth difficult. You can buy a harmonica with a little introductory bundle clarifying the design encased in the container. What is important to know is that everything is as of now set up in the chords. You have to play most sorts of music on a Richter, or ten-opening diatonic, harp, which offers you the chance to select fundamental tunes when you have a go at playing the harmonica for the first run through. Having the fundamental information, you can without much of a stretch improve your abilities by consistently working on playing this lovely instrument. The chance that you have as of now took in the nuts and bolts, and then you should seriously mull over getting some expert assistance. Obviously, you can begin taking harmonica exercises by a teacher, or you can basically begin tuning in to harmonica music played by other musicians. Music is said to be the best teacher, so why not check out the subsequent choice. On the off chance that you do as such, you will get numerous new thoughts and notwithstanding that playing the harmonica may empower you to give your own musical articulations which will be signified your collection. In the event that you choose to get a harmonica teacher to confirm that they are specialists in playing precisely the same style that you need. For example, envision you figured out how to play the harmonica in the Chicago chimes mode, then you would not have the option to play twang or nation blues harp as they all are altogether different styles.

Know your Harmonica

Every harmonica has a letter composed on it. The letter speaks to the key it is tuned to. Harmonica tuning utilizes the Richter tuning framework, so you can play chords that sound correct on the scale you play.

The accompanying table portrays the notes that 10-opening diatonic harmonicas will sound at each gap, in view of the key of your harmonica (positive numbers are for blowing, negative are for drawing).

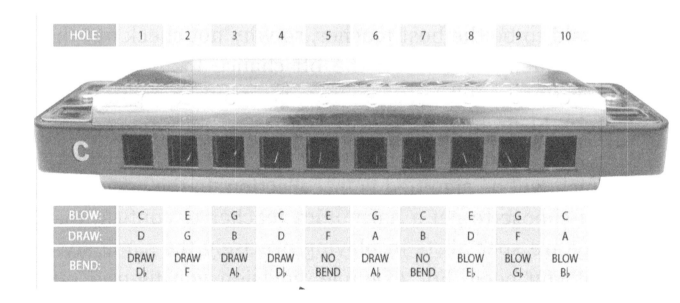

Key	1	-1	2	-2	3	-3	4	-4	5	-5	6	-6	7	-7	8	-8	9	-9	10	-10
C	C	D	E	G	G	B	C	D	E	F	G	A	C	B	E	D	G	F	C	A
Db	Db	Eb	F	Ab	Ab	C	Db	Eb	F	Gb	Ab	Bb	Db	C	F	Eb	Ab	Gb	Db	Bb
D	D	E	F#	A	A	C#	D	E	F#	G	A	B	D	C#	F#	E	A	G	D	B
Eb	Eb	F	G	Bb	Bb	D	Eb	F	G	Ab	Bb	C	Eb	D	G	F	Bb	Ab	Eb	C
E	E	F#	G#	B	B	D#	E	F#	G#	A	B	C#	E	D#	G#	F#	B	A	E	C#

F	F	G	A	C	C	E	F	G	A	Bb	C	D	E	E#	A	G	C	Bb	F	D
F#	F#	G#	A#	C#	C#	E#	F#	G#	A#	B	C#	D#	F	E	A#	G#	C#	B	F#	D#
G	G	A	B	D	D	F#	G	A	B	C	D	E	G	F#	B	A	D	C	G	E
Ab	Ab	Bb	C	Eb	Eb	G	Ab	Bb	C	Db	Eb	F	Ab	G	C	Bb	Eb	Db	Ab	F
A	A	B	C#	E	E	G#	A	B	C#	D	E	F#	A	G#	C#	B	E	D	A	F#
Bb	Bb	C	D	F	F	A	Bb	C	D	Eb	F	G	Bb	A	D	C	F	Eb	Bb	G
B	B	C#	D#	F#	F#	A#	B	C#	D#	E	F#	G#	B	A#	D#	C#	F#	E	B	G#

Music Notation with Tablature

Like guitars, harmonicas can be played by following sheet music, which decreases the notes on a sheet of music down to a simple-to-follow arrangement of holes and breath designs. Sheet music is valuable for bigger chromatic harmonicas too. However, it varies to some degree from diatonic sheet music and is less normal.

Breathing is set apart by bolts. An up bolt demonstrates a breath out; a down bolt shows a breath in.

Most holes on a diatonic harmonica produce two "neighbour" notes on a given scale; in this way playing C and afterwards, D on a similar scale is cultivated by blowing into the proper gap and afterwards attracting from a similar opening.

Holes are set apart with a number, beginning from the most minimal (left-hand) tone and moving upward. Subsequently, the most minimal two notes are (up) 1 and (down) 1. On a 10-gap harp, the most elevated note would be (down) 10.

A few notes on a normal 10-opening harmonica cover, eminently (down) 2 and (up) 3. This is important to permit an appropriate range for playing scales.

More propelled techniques are set apart with cuts or another little imprint. Corner to corner cuts through the bolts demonstrate that note bending (covered later) is required to get the best possible tone. Chevrons or slices on chromatic sheet music can likewise demonstrate whether or not to hold the catch in.

There is definitely not an institutionalized arrangement of sheet music that is utilized by all harmonica players. Be that as it may, when you rehearse and get comfortable perusing one sort, most other types will sound good to you rapidly.

Sheet music is a music notation method for a particular instrument. There are numerous sheet music frameworks for the harmonica. Right now will utilize the accompanying sign shows:

- A positive number (p.e. 5 or +5) implies you need to blow on that opening.
- A negative number (p.e. - 5) implies you need to draw on that gap.
- A number that is bigger than 10 is a chord. For instance, 12 is the chord of blowing in holes 1 and 2 at the same time, - 567 is a draw of holes 5, 6 and 7, etc. This method is for 10-opening diatonic harmonicas, so this notation isn't an issue. For

harmonicas (generally chromatic) that have more than 10 holes, other notation frameworks are utilized.

- A number with a statement (p.e. 5') implies you need to play on that gap considerably bending the note (you will get familiar with this procedure later on).
- A number with a twofold statement (p.e. 5") implies you need to play on that gap by full-bending the note (you will gain proficiency with this procedure later on).
- A number with a triple statement (p.e. 5''') implies you need to play on that gap by over-bending the note (you will gain proficiency with this procedure later on).

Rests will be noted as a blow on opening zero (0).

The large issue with scores is that note length, and extraordinary techniques are not noted.

Right now will utilize an extra line to show you the length of the note. In the planning line, the length will be:

/1   for an entire note

/2   for a half note

/4   for a quarter note etc

Do note will be recorded with an oblique punctuation line (\) rather than a slice.

Staccato (flashing playing a note, and afterwards stopping for its remainder time esteem) will be documented with a spot (.) rather than a cut.

Slide (a method indicated later on) will be recorded with an equivalent sign (=) at the tab line. Shake (a system demonstrated later on) will be recorded with a twist (~) at the tab line.

An or more sign (+) will take note of the expansion of multiple times. For instance, /2+/8 methods you need to play the note for a large portion of the note, and ceaselessly, you should keep on playing the note for an extra eighth note.

Blowing a harmonica/How to Hold Your harmonica

There are two methods of playing the harp; the Pucker method and the tongue blocking method. The two ways of playing are exact, neither is more adequate than the other in spite of the fact that blues folks will in general favour tongue hindering for a usual blues style. At the point when you become more experienced, you ought to have the option to switch comfortably between the two. Be that as it may, start with the one that feels normal to you, continue rehearsing the one that appears to be strange to you as it'll, in the long run, need acing on the off chance that you are to get heavenly with the harp! None of the two styles is anything but difficult to ace promptly; you would require heaps of training to do as such, however with time, it will drop into spot, and you'll have its hang, simply show restraint. There are loads of recordings on Youtube that can help with these techniques that a ton of tenderfoot blues harp players find valuable.

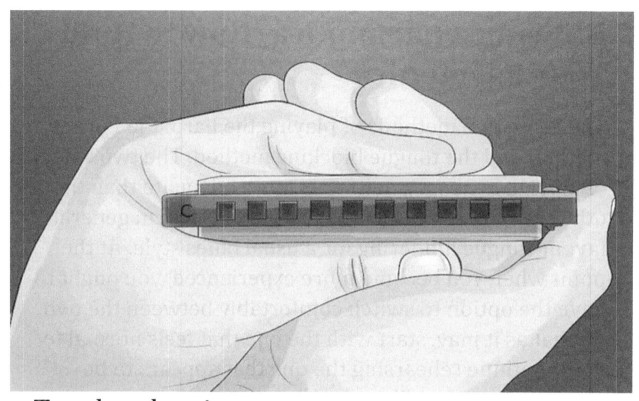

Two hands grip

If you have large hands

Step by step instructions to put the harmonica in your mouth

- At the point when you're holding the harp by its finishes, put it in your mouth with these means:
- Open your mouth wide like you need to yawn.
- Utilize your forearms to carry the harmonica to your open mouth.
- Spot the harmonica between your lips until it contacts the corners of your mouth; where your top and base lips meet.
- Delicately close your lips over the cover.

A Tip for playing, Do not move your head along the harmonica, instead, move the harmonica.

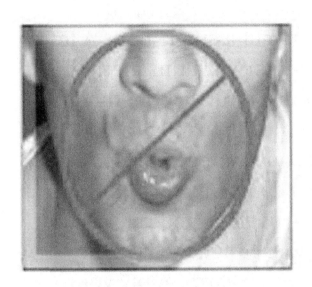 

DON'T DO THIS **DO THIS**

Puckering

Puckering is the usual method to start playing. It includes narrowing your lips to get a single note. A lot of new understudies become familiar with this method first, and it is absolutely the most effortless method for the two ways to deal with handle blow and draw twists. To pucker, with a snappy lick, guarantee your lips are, tighten your lips as you would do when whistling, this would make a gap. Loosen up your lips and release up marginally. Utilize the tip of your tongue to find the opening you need to play and afterwards apply your pucker directly around the harp. Stall out in.

To play, breathe out delicately and push from your stomach; Inhale tenderly, pulling from your chest and stomach.

It is alright on the off chance that you hear more than one note from the start, notwithstanding, work on playing single holes. Continue working on, tuning in and figuring out how to change your pucker until you can limit the sound.

Tongue Blocking

In tongue square, you get a single note by covering 3-4 holes with your mouth and utilize your tongue to cover (or "square") everything except one. In the event that puckering comes to you usually, blocking would set aside a great deal of effort to. It is, in any case, perfect for picking up blocking in the event that you wish to get that considerable tone and to give your sound a stout quality. Tongue slapping, chord and mood backup, vacillating, octaving and a ton of other incredible impacts opens up once you split this method and fundamental for blues harmonica, however, be cautioned it is an expertise that takes a great deal of time, years as a rule.

Breath Control; Blowing and Drawing Notes

"Blowing" and "Drawing" are the terms used to depict how notes are played on the harmonica. You have to consider blow and draw as breathe in and breathe out to get sublime tones when you play the harmonica. You don't puff at a harmonica; instead, you breathe out through it. You additionally don't suck air through a harmonica; you breathe in through it. Like singing, all high harmonica notes originate from the stomach. Never overdraw or overblow when playing! A great deal of amateurs frequently go over the edge and put a lot of air into it. Playing a harmonica genuinely needn't bother with a ton of air to get an extraordinary sound.

The harmonica reacts well to the negligible measure of air developments. On the off chance that you need more volume than the harmonica gives typically, rather than blowing harder to get it, get a receiver and speaker.

Techniques for Playing

What's more, presently comes an issue that many are starting harmonica players experience. You take a gander at the diagram on the past advance, say, "That appears to be sufficiently simple," blow into your harmonica, and three notes turn out. Here are how to simply play one note.

There are two primary methods:

Pucker method: To play this way, start with your lips loose. If you breathe out or breathe in, you will hear numerous notes. Presently push your lips outward, as though you were attempting to kiss somebody. The investigation until you can get a single, bright sign. Currently remain that way. It might be useful to think about your lips as being finished or around the harmonica, rather than just on it. If you remove the harp, and you look silly, you're doing it right.

This may appear to be hard from the start, yet once you get its hang (which shouldn't take long), it's a powerful method.

Tongue method: Relax your mouth, so it is covering various holes, then cover the ones you don't need with your tongue. This method is frequently used to "split" notes, permitting you to play two letters that aren't legitimately beside one another by placing your tongue in the middle of them.

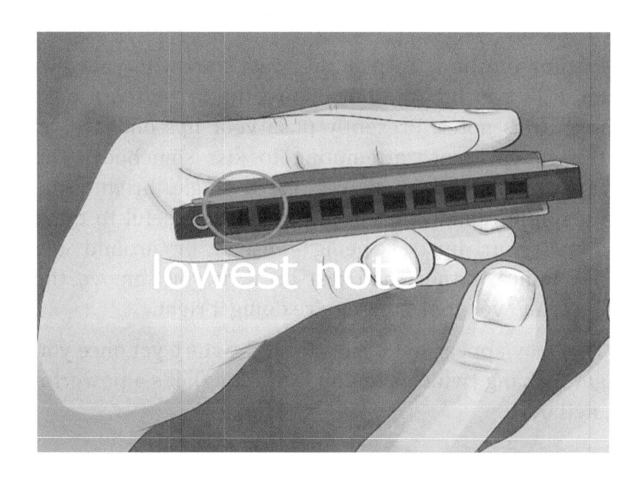

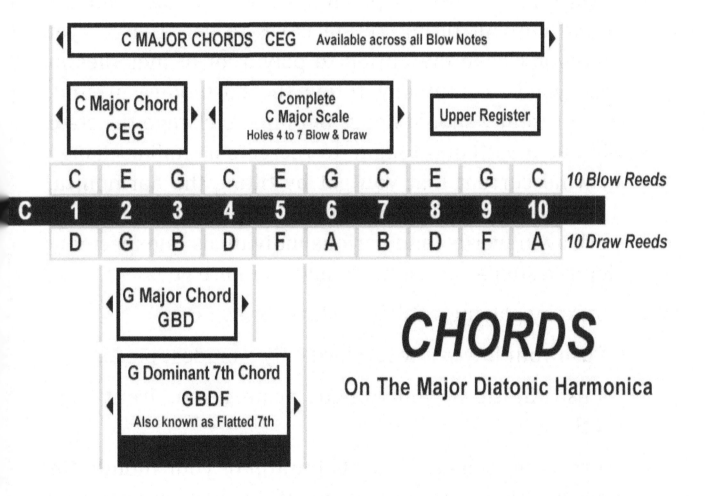

Playing "twists" Without Tilting the Harmonica (prescribed)

After you have arrived at the purpose of having the option to get "twists" utilizing the tilting method, its opportunity to begin figuring out how to get a similar sound without tilting, tilting is OK to get "twists", yet you won't have the option to play a lot of melodies in case you're continually tilting the harmonica around. You presently should figure out how to change the state of your mouth and tongue to recreate a similar change in wind current that you got by tilting the harmonica. This is the most troublesome harmonica system to portray in words (and various individuals unexpectedly depict a similar procedure) however here goes.

- Start by playing a solitary, clean, draw note.

- Push your lower jaw forward only a modest piece.

- Push the tip of your tongue against your front base teeth.

- Arch your tongue towards the top of your mouth. (in any case, don't curve such a lot of that you remove your airflow).

- Draw (pull the air) somewhat harder to make up for the sharp wind stream edge brought about by your jaw and tongue changes.

- Caution: Don't draw excessively hard or you will move past "draw twist" to "overdraw twist".

- Do 2,3,4, and 5 as near at the same time as could be expected under the circumstances.

- Listen for the adjustment in pitch (the "twist").

- Congratulations!

- Immediately after the curve, loosen up your jaw loosen up your tongue

- Return your tongue to its customary spot (at the base of your mouth)

Proceed with the draw, and the note should come back to its standard clean single note sound.

There you have it. "Bending" a note just requires two things: great breath control and the capacity to "move" or change the wind current.

The following is a chart of which notes can and can't be twisted.

Playing in Different Positions

Your harmonica may have more than one key imprinted on it. On one side it likely says C, however on the other side, it may state G. Which key is it in? Your harmonica is actually in C. However, and you can play an alternate sort of scale in the key of G.

The regular situation of the harmonica (right now, the key of C) is called first position or straight harp. The second position, or cross harp, is the key a fifth up from first position (G).

Why utilize various positions? Two reasons. To begin with, they permit you to play in numerous keys on one harmonica. Second, it permits both of you to play scales other than the standard major scale. For instance, on the off chance that I needed to play a blues scale in C, I would utilize a harmonica in the key of F.

Each position is a fifth up from the following. In this way, on a C harmonica, the first position would be in the key of C, second in G, third in D, fourth in An, and fifth in E. You will once in a while use anything past the fifth position, and you will ordinarily adhere to 1, 2, and 4.

How To Play The Diatonic Harmonica In The Key of C:

1. Hold the harmonica with one hand at each end, with the numbers facing you. Low notes are on the left and high notes are on the right

2. Holes 4, 5, 6 and 7 will play the notes of the beginner songs.

3. Position your mouth over the fourth hole. Pretend you are sipping on a

straw, or whistling.

4. Blowing into hole 4 will play a C. Draw on hole 4 and you have D.

5. Blowing into hole 5 plays an E. Drawing out plays F.

6. Blow on 6 for a G and draw to get A.

7. Draw on 7 for a B.

8. Blow into 7 for the top note of the C major scale.

9. Practice going slowly up and down the scale several times until you can touch any note.

10. Lift your tongue on and off holes 1, 2 and 3 and you will get a C chord.

Make sure your mouth is clean before playing. Tap the harmonica lightly to remove debris. Soaking your harmonica in water is NOT recommended.

Frequently Asked Questions

Should I have the option to peruse music to play the harmonica?

No. There are a few frameworks for documenting harmonica music that doesn't utilize a clef. Most go through bolts for the blow (breathe out) notes, and down pins for the draw (breath in) notes.

Consider the possibility that I have issues playing a single note.

Try not to worry a lot about playing single notes. Have some good times with the tunes first. Practice individual letters by putting your pointers firmly over holes 3 and 5 and pack the entire thing into your mouth. Tightly cover holes 3 and 5 and practice blowing into opening 4. Or, utilize your fingers to physically crush in the corners of your lips. Presently attempt to keep up this situation without your thumbs. The average individual takes half a month to get this procedure. Rehash it gradually again and again until you assemble the correct muscle memory.

How far in my mouth should the harmonica go?

The harmonica ought to consistently be between your lips and not against them. That is, we need the harp against within our mouths and not the outside of our lips. Give this a shot gap number 4, gradually blowing and drawing. When in doubt, consistently put the harmonica as far into your mouth as could be expected under the circumstances while as yet playing a spotless single note.

To what extent would it be a good idea for me to practice?

For the initial barely any long stretches of playing, you will locate that after a short measure of time your lips get worn out, and they don't do precisely what you ask them to. This is consummately normal and will leave with practice and time. It is usual for your mouth and hands to get drained subsequent to playing for broadened periods. Practice for 10 minutes 2 or 3 times each day and develop your perseverance.

Imagine a scenario in which the harmonica adheres to my lips.

If your lips start adhering to the harmonica when you go from gap to gap, lick your lips and the portion of the harmonica where you would put them. Any oils other than your usual spit are not prescribed.

Shouldn't something be said about salivation?

Keep your head up while playing, which will help keep the abundance spit that you will typically produce from winding up in the harmonica. Expel abundance dampness from inside the harmonica every once in a while, by rapping the harmonica, mouthpiece down, against your palm or leg. The abundance dampness can obstruct the reeds in the harmonica.

Practice Exercises

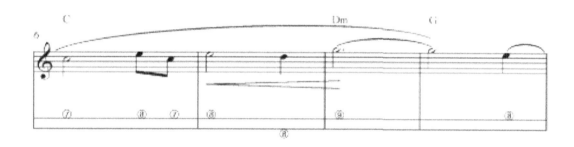

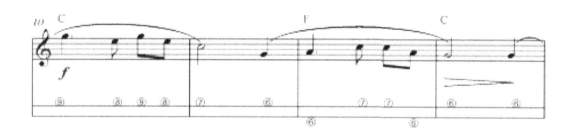

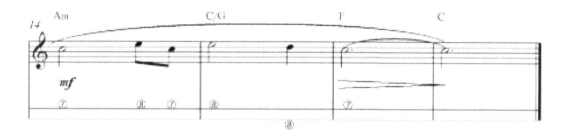

Deck the Halls (C Harmonica)

Danse des lauriers verts

Initialement en do majeur

Trad.

Y a dix corbeaux

Trad.

Books by the same author:

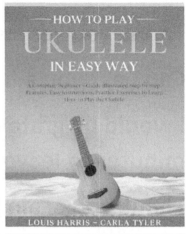
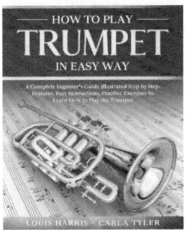

Search: "Louis Harris"
on Amazon

Kind reader,

Thank you very much. I hope you enjoyed the book.

Can I ask you a big favor?

I would be grateful if you would please take a few minutes to leave me a gold star on Amazon.

Thank you again for your support.

Louis Harris

Made in the USA
Las Vegas, NV
17 January 2024

84490077R00033